"G.S. Merriam must have had Herb Stansbury in mind when he said, 'The sense of humor is the oil of life's engine. Without it, the machinery creaks and groans. No lot is so hard, no aspect of things is so grim, but it relaxes before a hearty laugh.' STANSBURY'S SMART CHARTS, WITH THEIR MIXTURE OF WIT, HUMOR, AND IRREVERENCE, ARE A WELCOME ANTIDOTE TO THESE OFTEN DIFFICULT AND UNCERTAIN TIMES. TO LAUGH IS TO LIVE . . . AND PROBABLY A LITTLE LONGER TOO!"

> John G. Goode
> President & CEO
> Davis Skaggs Investment Management

"I've known Herb Stansbury for years as a marketing expert, friendly banker, business speaker, and cartoonist. What else? And now his fine, funny book about boardroom absurdity and the laughter deficit. 'GENTLE LAUGHTER AND A SENSE OF HUMOR ARE ESSENTIAL INGREDIENTS TO GOOD COMMUNICATION AND LEADERSHIP,' SAYS HERB. I AGREE."

> Walter A. Haas, Jr.,Honorary Chairman
> Levi-Strauss & Co.
> Owner, Oakland A's

"ANYONE WHO KNOWS HERB STANSBURY KNOWS WHAT TO EXPECT. He has a delightful way of making you look at yourself as you appear to others. The art of humor is a friendly gig—just a nudge and never a push. In these skills, Herb excels."

> William R. Hewlett
> Hewlett-Packard Company

"HERB STANSBURY'S CHARTS MAY NOT HELP YOU BECOME A FINANCIAL GURU OR BILLIONAIRE . . . I'M NOT SURE . . . BUT THEY WILL LIGHTEN THE WAY THROUGH YOUR BUSINESS LIFE."

> Richard B. Madigan, Captain
> The Highlanders

"IT'S DIFFICULT TO EXPLAIN HERB IN A FEW WORDS. Create, write, sell, humor, cartoon, talk, laugh, people, affection, ideas, imagination, brain, profit, focus, and entrepreneur are some I would use. Any order or combination works."

> David L. Maggard, Director of Sports
> Atlanta Committee for the Olympic Games

"To humble the pompous boardroom image with cartoon humor created by someone who has been there is good medicine, I'd say. I GRINNED MY WAY THROUGH HERB STANSBURY'S BOOK."

> Denny A. McLeod, President & CEO
> Rigging International

"STANSBURY DELIVERS UNIQUE COMIC RE-LIEF OF THE HIGHEST ORDER. He says it like it is. Like it REALLY is."

> James E. Wickersham, President
> Triangle T Ranch

EXECUTIVE
SMART CHARTS
& OTHER INSIDER REVELATIONS
ON CORPORATE INSANITY

by

H E R B   S T A N S B U R Y

Board Chairman &
Nationally Syndicated Cartoonist

■ ■ ■

Berrett-Koehler Publishers
San Francisco

Berrett-Koehler Publishers, Inc.
155 Montgomery St.
San Francisco, CA 94104-4109
Tel: 415-288-0260   Fax: 415-362-2512

Ordering Information
Individual sales. Berrett-Koehler publications are available through most bookstores. They can also be ordered direct from Berrett-Koehler at the address above.
Quantity sales. Special discounts are available on quantity purchases by corporations, associations, and others. For details, contact the "Special Sales Department" at the Berrett-Koehler address above.
Orders for college textbook/course adoption use. Please contact Berrett-Koehler Publishers at the address above.
Orders by U. S. trade bookstores and wholesalers. Please contact Publishers Group West, P.O. Box 8843, Emeryville, CA 94662;
510-658-3453; 1-800-788-3123.

Printed in the United States of America

Printed on acid-free and recycled paper that meets the strictest state and U.S. guidelines for recycled paper (50 percent recycled waste, including 10 percent postconsumer waste).

Library of Congress Cataloging-in-Publication Data
Stansbury, Herb. 1925-
    Executive smart charts & other insider revelations on corporate insanity / by Herb Stansbury. — 1st ed.
        p. cm.
    ISBN 1-881052-37-0 (hardcover alk. paper) — ISBN 1-881052-36-2 (paperback: alk. paper)
      1. Corporations — Management — Charts, diagrams, etc. — Caricatures and cartoons. 2. American wit and humor. Pictorial. I. Title. II. Title: Executive smart charts and other insider revelations on corporate insanity.
      NC1429.S572A4 1993   93-27144
      741.5'973 — dc20   CIP

First Edition
  First Printing 1993

Cover Design by Robb Pawlak
Book Design by Dianne Platner

For Audrey—my wife, who loves me as much as I love her, and backed me cheerfully through a 36-month gestation period while I put this together.

"When you are bored stiff with meetings and business-talk, cartoon doodling is what you do to maintain your sanity," she once observed with precision.

Dennis Green, Ted Michel, and Margot Smith Chmel are the wise owls who examined many pounds of my paper scraps, gave advice, and cheered me on. My special thanks to them, my family, close friends, and publisher, who made this project such a happy undertaking.

Table of Contents

Preface

If you read my book, you will not begin to invest more wisely, become a marketing wizard, dress differently, or get organized for economic doomsday.

There are no references to dead economists, no one-minute solutions, and no high-technology computer-as-human-brain metaphors. Nor are there any case studies or spread sheets. It is fast, cheerful reading.

Instead of conventional business props, I use cartoons to make my points, but don't let this mislead you. This is a serious book written for men and women who are very serious about their careers, but don't take themselves seriously. I use cartoons because they provide the most direct access to truth and because cartoons are the most efficient graphic medium.

Most simply stated, this book has to do with talking straight. Telling the truth. Saying it like it really is. That's all.

Most of my adult life I have lived as a businessman and at the same time as a syndicated cartoonist. I hang out with business people. I enjoy business people. I belong to their clubs. I am one of them. In fact, I am chairman of a multibillion dollar company.

But under my skin I am still a cartoonist and perhaps that qualifies me as some breed of humorist, uniquely equipped to give others a sense of what it is really like to be there in the corporate boardrooms and executive suites and to witness some of the wonderful absurdities I've stumbled across in my search for the truth.

The most I can hope for is that you will smile, possibly laugh, and feel as though you have taken a step toward reaffirming your business sanity.

It is also my wish that in the future you will approach all business-related communication with the wonderful anticipation you once reserved for the funny papers.

Herbert E. Stansbury, Jr.

Piedmont, California
September 1993

Chapter 1

Doodling Up the Corporation

**Humor provides the
most direct access to truth.**

Introduction

I have drawn cartoons as long as I can remember. While Miss Jerome, my earliest baby-sitter, read *Uncle Wiggly* to me, I occupied myself with Crayolas and soft-lead Ticonderoga pencils. I drew and wrote on everything, including walls and window sills. Eventually I was converted to Big Chief drawing tablets, butcher paper, and shirt cardboards.

Drawing cartoons on the backs of bank statements and canceled checks bothered my parents a lot. They didn't appreciate having the family's financial paper circulated around El Paso adorned with Krazy Kat, Chester Gump, and Moon Mullins, plus the Spads, Sopwith Camels, and Fokker D VII's of World War I.

Ignatz, the brick-throwing mouse from George Herriman's wonderful "Krazy Kat" was a special pal. I drew him over and over. I still do. "Demon of Anarchy" and "Champion of Free Will" is how e. e. cummings described him.

Many worshipped the cat. I worshipped the miserable mouse.

I am still grateful to the old State National Bank of El Paso, my most reliable source of high-rag-content, quality drawing paper during the Great Depression.

Today, more than a half century later, I still draw with enthusiasm and have a unique, comfortable place to do it. I am alone there, it is quiet, and my brain works at a relaxed tempo. There are no interruptions, no regulators, no bureaucrats, no politicians. I call it "My secret world of ironic business humor and cartoons."

It's physical location can by anywhere, but generally it is the den off the bedroom or at my workbench in the basement. Sometimes it's right where I'm sitting at the boardroom table. When I am home, I go to the den very early, about 3 a.m., to write, draw, read, and reflect about sex, satire, dinosaurs, deficits, business, and absurdities in general.

The discovery of my secret world occurred much in the manner that Alice discovered the rabbit hole under the hedge. It was at the Waldorf-Astoria, midmorning, 24 years ago during a dull corporate meeting of shareholders (not mine). I had drifted into a bored, relaxed reverie-fantasy when up popped a bright idea. Just like the white rabbit.

Here's what happened:

The company had some extremely difficult things to explain to its stockholders . . . why a merger went bad, costly litigation, declining sales, product failures, and not enough reserved for bad debts.

What could the President say? Would he be chased down Park Avenue? Maybe hung in effigy?

After brief, amiable, introductory remarks, he projected the following chart on a huge screen and made the comment which became the caption for my first Smart Chart.

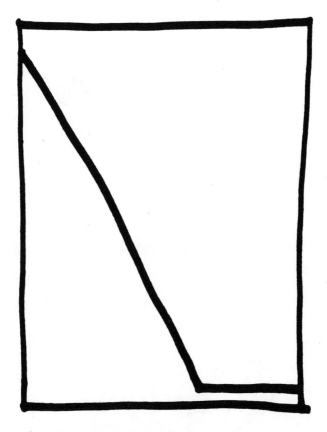

It was a year of challenge and change
. . . however we successfully constructed
a platform base from which future
earnings may be soundly projected.

I had difficulty restraining laughter, but the crowd remained silent and showed no emotion.

Charts are useful tools in such situations because the average audience feels that something sophisticated and possibly beyond its understanding has taken place. They don't want to risk asking a stupid question in front of strangers. In this instance it would have been impossible for a stockholder to have made a comment dumber than the CEO's. At that instant I knew I had my first Smart Chart.

Charts also have a subtle hypnotic effect. There's a little mystery. This conservative, older group of stockholders had been served juice, tea, coffee, and big tollhouse cookies, plus a lavish four-color annual report that could have won an award for fiction.

The Chief Financial Officer didn't do as well. He was a cheerful, brilliant-looking combination Harvard-MBA-CPA-attorney with a pencil-thin neck and a collection of transparencies that didn't project well. He had lots of charts, about 12 too many, and typography that was not readable past the third row.

Chief Financial Officers love charts but frequently use more than are necessary. They have a tendency to jam too much into each chart and use too many lines. The best charts are simple, with just one or two lines. Sometimes three. This was the CFO's first chart and the caption is his exact words:

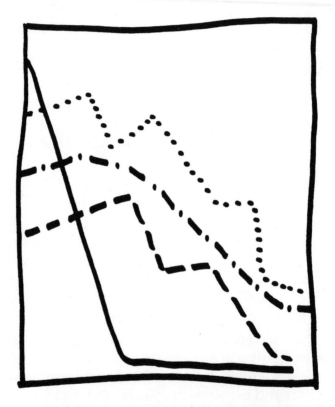

Only the sophisticated investor will appreciate what our progress has been in areas other than financial.

Forwards, backwards, or sideways, what he had said made no sense, but it seemed OK with everyone. The chart was a disaster-scene landscape. I believe I knew what he wanted to say, but he didn't say it.

He might have said, "Our recent financial performance has been rotten for a lot of reasons. Let me explain why." That would have made sense and his candor would have been appreciated. Although financial performance had been terrible, it was not because of frail or incompetent management. He could have explained this quickly and gone

THEY DIDN'T SMILE ←

THE BOARD CHAIRMAN   THE PRESIDENT

on to describe the company's breakthroughs in R&D which looked exciting and financially attractive.

The Chief Financial Officer didn't do as well as the President and the crowd eventually got around to abusing him a bit. I suspect he never used his opening slide again. The Chairman didn't smile and neither did the President. I suppressed a chuckle as I scribbled my second Smart Chart on a Waldorf-Astoria envelope.

The "take charge," prematurely white-haired marketing Vice President had some friendly warm-up words and projected this chart to explain a disappointing sales year:

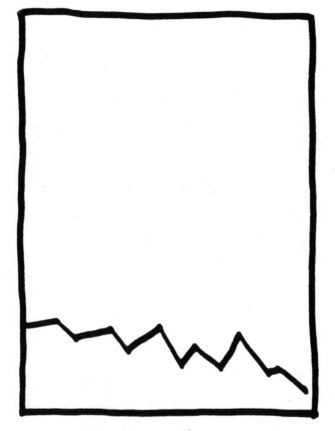

**We do not believe in
irresponsible sales growth.**

It didn't work! The audience was quiet for a moment until an attractive Barbara Bush-type lady from Tenafly, New Jersey stood, and with a smile said, "Might you be induced to believe in a teeny-weeny bit of responsible growth?"

Her question ignited the crowd, laughter followed, and the questions flew for more than an hour. The cookies, tea, and coffee were all gone when the crowd filed out later, but half of the colorful annual reports had been left behind. The Waldorf-Astoria experience altered my business life in a wonderful way.

Although I had drawn pictures and captions on envelopes, scratch pads, and menus for years, the experience of seeing fellow business executives in action with their incredible charts suggested a new concept in business humor. A new way to get at the truth.

Back in San Francisco, my pockets full of captions, I was fired up by the idea of becoming a syndicated cartoonist. I phoned the presidents of five newspaper syndicates and within one week negotiated a five-year contract with Rex Barley, President of the Los Angeles Times Syndicate at that time.

As with most endeavors, simplicity is best. "Don't get complex or cute," Rex Barley reminded me. "Cuteness and complexity are enemies of good humor and usually kill the joke."

Rex hammered on the theme of creative quality and the hard work of sustaining something *daily* for the rest of one's life.

To test my sustaining ability, Rex asked for 60 more Smart Chart panels within the week. To show off I sent him 120. He discarded ten and I passed.

How to Draw Smart Charts

There is an inclination among adults to regard doodling as a childhood activity. It may begin in childhood, but most doodlers doodle into old age. As far back as I can remember, I have doodled, drawn, cartooned, and sketched. Over time my doodles became more refined and evolved into Smart Charts.

Following is the procedure for creating your own Smart Charts. A wonderful activity to help you maintain your sanity through dull meetings.

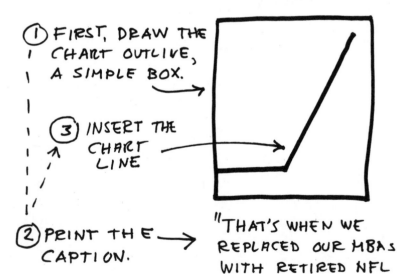

① FIRST, DRAW THE CHART OUTLINE, A SIMPLE BOX.

③ INSERT THE CHART LINE

② PRINT THE CAPTION. → "THAT'S WHEN WE REPLACED OUR MBAs WITH RETIRED NFL LINEBACKERS."

Thinking of captions is obviously the most significant part. Distill your message to the fewest possible words. Be certain the chart line and caption are perfectly synchronized.

Theatrically speaking, the chart is a proscenium arch and the chart lines are props. The captions are the voices of the actors or Greek chorus offstage. That's how I think of it.

The question cartoonists are asked often is "Where do you get your captions?"

There are many good sources for Smart Chart captions. Financial news services and annual reports trigger lots of ideas. Attorneys, accountants, and financial consultants spew forth caption material constantly. Those professions have a built-in stuffiness factor that makes for a ton of funny talk every day. Other occupations also spin off good grist for captions—politicians, high bureaucrats, athletic team managers, coaches, and academic researchers are a few.

At the meeting of a big utility company in San Francisco recently, the CEO was asked by a former employee why so many hundreds had been fired.

"Now we are a leaner, meaner organization building a stronger foundation for dividend growth," was the precise reply. Then he moved quickly on to the next question.

Many believe that we live in an age of overcommunication. I don't agree. I believe we live in an age of massive undercommunication, complicated by the overtransmission of garbage.

By "garbage" I mean bad language, bad grammar, shocking graphics, and general swill, much of it presented to us by the smarmy, cutesy, newsreader teams.

Doodling Smart Charts is my friendly response to the environment as I thrash my way through the jungle of mass media and communication despair.

A simple cartoon, boldly presented, with an honest caption, may be the most efficient system for revealing truth . . . "telling it like it is."

Casually doodled Smart Charts by senior executives are fine aids to legitimate communication in this era of dumb, bad talk.

Following is a group of the original Smart Charts which led to syndication. Perhaps they will inspire you to create some of your own.

SMART CHART

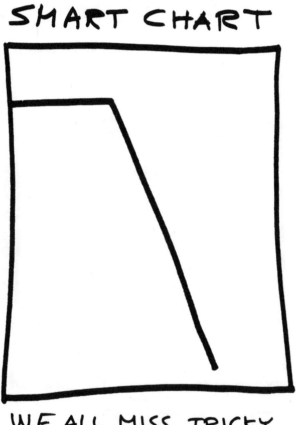

WE ALL MISS TRICKY
BEN IN ACCOUNTING.

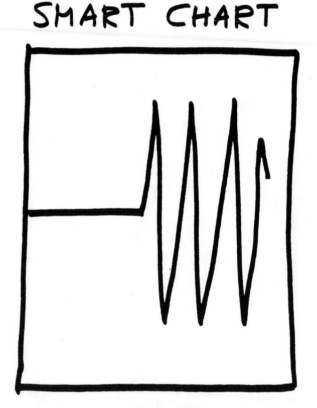

SMART CHART

THE MERGER'S NOT
GOING QUITE AS
WE ANTICIPATED.

SMART CHART

WE DIDN'T RESERVE
ENOUGH FOR BAD DEBTS.

SMART CHART

WE HAVE AN ACCOUNTING PROBLEM... WE RAN OUT OF MONEY.

SMART CHART

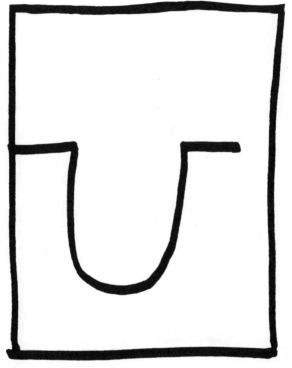

IT WAS GREAT HAVING
YOUR SON WITH US
THIS SUMMER, CHIEF.

SMART CHART

HAS ANYONE NOTICED THAT
THIS IS THE FIFTH YEAR
OF OUR FIVE-YEAR PLAN?

SMART CHART

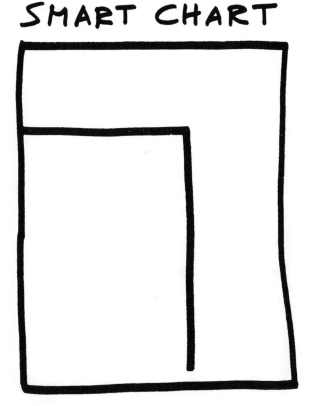

THAT'S WHEN THEY
DISCOVERED OUR SEWER
LINE INTO THE LAKE.

SMART CHART

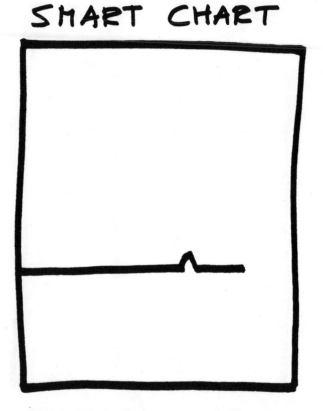

RESPONSE TO THE
CHAIRMAN'S MESSAGE
WAS RESTRAINED.

SMART CHART

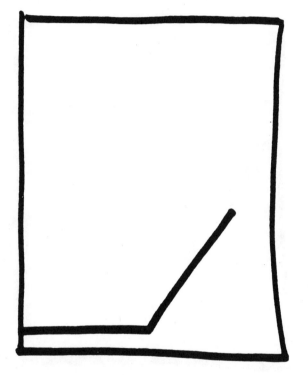

WE FOUND WE COULD
GRIND OUR NUCLEAR WASTE
AND SELL IT AS TRAIL MIX.

SMART CHART

MAYBE WE OUGHT TO
DIVERSIFY OUT OF
DAIRY PRODUCTS.

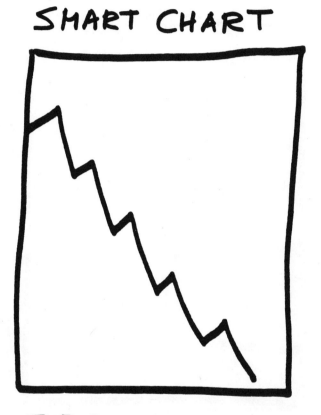

SMART CHART

THE GOOD NEWS IS WE
GOT THROUGH THE YEAR
AND WEREN'T INDICTED.

SMART CHART

STEP IN HERE A MINUTE,
CLIFFORD... I WANT TO
SPEAK WITH YOU ABOUT
YOUR EXPENSE ACCOUNT.

SMART CHART

GOOD NEWS IS JUST
AROUND THE CORNER...
WE'RE NOT SURE OF
THE PRECISE LOCATION.

Getting Animated

Rex Barley, President of the L.A. Times Syndicate, was a good man, full of wit and upbeat spirit. He had been a war correspondent and wore a trench coat with all the loops and buckles for military hardware. An old Burberry coat.

We got into an every-other-month lunch cycle, usually in Los Angeles, but once in a while in San Francisco in the Pied Piper Room

of the Palace Hotel. Rex liked Maxfield Parrish's "Pied Piper" painting behind the bar.

One day, over lunch at the Los Angeles Biltmore, when Smart Chart was about three years old, Rex asked if I knew how to draw people . . . "cartoon people." I had been thinking of myself as a unique combination business executive-cartoonist, and suddenly I realized that to Rex, Smart Chart was simply a chart. There were no cartoon characters, only chart lines and captions.

"Of course I can draw people cartoons," I replied, a little steamed. "I've been drawing cartoons all my life! If I'm not a cartoonist, what am I? How am I identified in the *L.A. Times* records? Anybody can be an executive. Cartoonists are rare. They're special. They make people laugh, smile, and feel good. When I die I want 'cartoonist' in my epitaph, not 'board chairman'!"

"I think I understand. For the record, you are identified on our records as a 'talent' and Smart Chart is a 'small brightener,' " Rex grinned. "We couldn't think of anything else. But we are open-minded, and beginning today you are a cartoonist, OK? But we feel that Smart Chart would be enlivened by the physical

introduction of some of your business pals
. . . executive types mostly. . . .

"Draw some board chairmen and CEOs along with financial types, and a few MBAs with their strategic plans. Be sure to include Ace Clifford, Tricky Ben, and those other characters who have been off camera until now. And don't overlook women in business. They'll be running everything soon."

I recalled that Rex's ultimate boss at the *L.A. Times* was Buffy Chandler, so he had had lots of experience in an environment of strong female leadership.

"No problem, Rex. I have a wife, mother, two daughters, three sisters, a secretary, and I know lots of women who feel the same way. I like women. No problem. I'll include all the others as well. No problem."

Rex's final comment as we walked back to my car was, "Why don't you send me a bunch of cartoon samples this week so we can get a notion of what to expect with the new Smart Charts, OK?"

As I drove out Century Boulevard to the airport, I had the strong impression that Rex did not think I could draw.

Following are samples of the first Smart Charts I drew with people—"cartoon people," as Rex called them. Now there were CEOs, platoons of vice presidents, accountants, attorneys, MBAs, and all kinds of executives, including nerds and wimps.

During that spate of mergers we accidentally acquired two small Latin American governments.

Sorry Goodman . . . no raise,
but the Board did vote you a
unanimous nice going.

It's not a bad performance when
one considers that not one of us
has given up the 3-Martini lunch.

FROM THE HEAD-WAITER MANUAL

① HOW TO GREET CUSTOMER.
② HOW TO REGARD CUSTOMER'S WINE SELECTION.
③ HOW TO ACKNOWLEDGE CUSTOMER'S TIP... AND DEPARTURE.

Your strategic plan, brilliant in
concept and magnificent in
execution, isn't working.

The Syndicate liked my scraps and for the next 12 years I produced Smart Charts six days a week while carrying on other business. "When you are bored stiff, you maintain your sanity by drawing cartoons," my wife Audrey quipped one evening on the way to San Francisco. My situation could not have been sized up with greater precision.

I enjoyed the new activity, made some new money, became a guest speaker on business humor, ran my other business affairs, enjoyed healthy laughter, was rarely bored, and had the satisfaction of sharing my views on business communication and corporate health.

From this point on, Smart Charts contained people . . . and charts, too, most of the time.

Doodle Research at Pebble Beach

Rich men, poor men, beggar men, and investment bankers doodle. The level of intelligence, education, and social sophistication means little. Einstein doodled. Churchill doodled. Heads of state doodle. Musicians doodle. Almost everyone doodles. Cave men doodled. Children doodle. Women doodle, but not as much.

I identify with those Cro-Magnon cave dwellers who decorated their walls at Lascaux, France, 20,000 years ago. Their art was early graffiti. Doodling. Drawing was a natural act for them.

FAKE LASCAUX - TYPE ART

It doesn't mean anything . . . all I
know is when the line goes up
everybody feels good.

I focused momentarily on the subject of doodling 22 years ago at a Pebble Beach seminar of international publishing executives. We arranged for each participant to have a large scratch pad and several sharp pencils with the program kit. Seating was arranged in a comfortable alignment that made doodling easy and private.

At the end of the day, I picked up the leftover pads and scattered pages. I identified each owner with his creative doodling and did my research.

I collected 123 pages and scraps of doodles from 72 participants. Some executives escaped with their artwork while others absent-mindedly destroyed theirs by tearing it into small bits or reducing it to spitballs. It was surprising that many were embarrassed when asked to discuss their creative efforts.

This is what my rough research revealed:

1. Big shots doodle as much as little shots. Men and women.

2. Doodle volume increases with meeting dullness. Dull speakers generate lots of doodling. You don't want to be a "High-Doodle" Speaker.

← "HIGH-DOODLE" SPEAKER

3. There was great artistic variety and variation in drawing skills. The scraps of one prominent CEO were primitive and those of his sales director were spectacular caricatures of those sitting nearby.

4. Many were secretive about their artwork and took pains to conceal it. I wondered about them. Others readily displayed their efforts, especially if they thought it funny.

SCATOLOGICAL DOODLER CONCEALING HIS ART

5. Geometric patterns were common. Lots of triangles, trapezoids, hexagons, and arrows. Not many sketches of people. And it was a surprise not to see more dollar signs. They were dollar-oriented people.

AGGRESSIVE ECONOMIST ABOUT
TO SNAP HIS LEAD THE
SECOND TIME.

6. The more aggressive executives pushed their pencils hard enough to groove the paper and occasionally snap the lead. A McGraw-Hill regional manager sitting next to me broke the lead in all three of his pencils.

Someday I will find an energetic MBA to continue my research. I have merely scratched the surface.

Chapter 2

Humor in and Around the Boardroom

O f all the qualities desired in a business leader, the one least talked about and most often overlooked is a sense of humor. By humor, I mean the wry sense of gentle irony which underlies everything we do.

Lately I've wondered what term Charles Darwin would use if he lived today. Would he use "survival of the dishonest," "survival of the scheming," or possibly "survival of the humorless?"

Massive financial deficits abound, but have you ever wondered if the humor deficit in our country is equally critical?

I emphasize good humor because it's such a terribly important ingredient of corporate good health. It's good for all employees, including board chairs, presidents, directors, and officers. In organizations where people don't laugh much (especially at themselves), extreme conservatism and corporate flat-footedness develop.

CHIEF FINANCIAL OFFICER, ON HIS TOES, FLEXIBLE, FEELING GOOD.

Good humor generally indicates that people are on their toes, flexible, feeling good, and better equipped to deal with change.

Without a sense of humor, people with power take themselves too seriously, egos blossom, and companies wither.

In my ongoing search for "corporate nonsense language," I meet many leaders who speak with precision and good humor. They don't generate Smart Charts but I love them because they appreciate my mission and laugh with me.

These are the qualities that distinguish them:

1. They laugh healthy laughter, not cynical or derisive laughter. They laugh at themselves.

2. They take their work seriously—not themselves.

3. They are skilled communicators. They write well and speak well and never obfuscate. They say it straight. The truth. No sugar-coating.

4. Each would make a fine role model.

But the majority persist with the dumb-funny language—speak it, write it in memos, and transmit it by all media.

Business leaders and those who aspire to leadership must understand the serious crime of needless words. William Strunk, Jr., the famous Cornell University English professor who wrote *The Elements of Style*, considered the use of needless words as almost felonious. He had this to say about brevity:

"Vigorous writing is concise. A sentence should contain no unnecessary words for the same reason a drawing should have no unnecessary lines and a machine no unnecessary parts. This requires not that the writer make all his sentences short or that he avoid all detail and treat his subjects only in outline, but that every word count."

I wonder how many CEOs Will Strunk would send to jail for their involvement with this year's crop of annual reports.

Fortunately, these reports reward us with lots of unintentional executive suite humor.

My special interest is in boardroom leaders who possess healthy senses of humor and other qualities worth emulating—authentic role models. Sol Linowitz, distinguished attorney and founding chairman of Xerox, is an example. Bill Hewlett of Hewlett Packard is another. Ditto for Wally Haas of Levi-Strauss and the Oakland A's, and so many more.

Warren Buffett of Berkshire Hathaway, Inc., is one of the finest practitioners of executive good humor I know. "You must laugh at yourself before anyone else can," insists Warren. He is one of the few top financier-executives who writes his own corporate messages to shareholders. He tells it exactly like it is and the reason he is so often funny is because the truth is so often funny.

I dwell on Warren Buffett because around boardrooms and among shareholders he is an

EXECUTIVES IN RESTROOM AT BEGINNING
OF DAY PRACTICE LAUGHING AT THEMSELVES
BEFORE ANYONE ELSE CAN.

active executive-financier who is the perfect combination of business acumen and good humor. I've often wondered if his humor portfolio is his greatest capital asset.

Warren and I became pen pals a few years ago when I lost my copy of the Berkshire Hathaway annual report and wrote for another. He responded promptly with two copies ("in case you lose one") and made some insightful comments about my own business. His candid messages in the annual report are superb examples of human communication.

In conversation with him about cartoon humor and our favorite comic strips, I learned that the late cartoonist Al Capp ranks high, perhaps alongside Benjamin Graham and David Dodd, as strong influences on the education of Warren Buffett.

Although Al Capp's Yokums were quaint hillbillies, they were a highly principled family with Pansy Yokum at the helm. A kind of morality play, with so many wonderful characters.

"Growing up I read 'Little Abner' every day and learned a lot about life. I miss Hairless Joe, Joe BTFSLK (the world's most loving friend and worst jinx), Marryn' Sam, Lonesome Polecat, Big Barnsmell, the Scragg Family, and all the rest," said Warren.

In order to give Warren some comic relief while he was absorbed with Salomon Brothers' problems, I sketched this Dogpatch-style cartoon on a yellow pad for him.

Warren - Keep up the good work -
8/21/91
MAMMY... AH MEMBERS THAT WUNNERFUL MR. BUFFETT WHO BRANG US DEELISHUS SEE'S CHOCOLATES WIF THE NICE OL' LADY ON THE BOX. DO HE NEED OUR HELP NOW?
YO IS MOS' THOUGHTFUL, SON. MR. BUFFETT IS JUS' FINE. IT TAKE STRONG MEN WIF CONFEEDENCE AN' INTEGRITEE LIKE HIS'N TO HELP THEM THAT IS NOT SO STRONG. HE WOULD BE PULEEZED TO KNOW YO IS THINKIN' OF HIM.
DOGPATCH GAZETTE
BUFFETT-CONT'D
(AND THANK YOU AL CAPP, WHEREVER YOU ARE)

Warren's response was pure Buffett. In thanking me for the message, he said that at that moment he would just as soon have Abner's first job right after he married Daisy Mae . . . mattress tester at the Little Wonder Mattress Factory in Dogpatch . . . hours 6 a.m. to 6 p.m., lying around on mattresses.

There is a lot of humor in and around boardrooms, but too much of it is accidental. We don't expect stand-up comedy from our corporate leaders, but we do look for signs of warmth, good humor, and human understanding. We search for leaders who talk straight, people with interesting ideas and intellect who can present a clearer vision of things.

If a bank doesn't have a few problem loans on the books, it's probably not doing its job.

SMART CHART
by Stansbury

Someone with inside
knowledge dumped our stock
and made a killing.

My sons don't understand
nepotism . . . they got control and
threw me out.

We must learn to face the
challenges of recession more
realistically.

I wonder if directors ever pretend
to be cleaning ladies.

We achieved a new high
in shareholder threats
successfully ignored.

**My grandson said his
first words—"tax shelter."**

Our problem is the competition . . .
they make better products and sell
them for less.

SMART CHART
by Stansbury

The only thing we do well
is keep score.

That's when we accidentally
shredded our strategic plan.

SMART CHART
by Stansbury

I have a great idea to discuss.
Bring in some yes-men.

This year, instead of plowing everything back into the organization, let's plow a little into our own pockets.

We loved your sermon on praying
for dividends, Father.

They all laughed at me and the little lamb that followed me to school one day until I became president of the International Wool Association.

I'm not sure our long-range
strategy is understood by those
who expected earnings this year.

We all know it's the board chairman's
big mouth . . . the real question is
which one of us is going to tell him.

I didn't say you were in financial trouble. I said you were morally bankrupt.

Sure, we've got a few problems . . . but
none that a favorable court decision
and a little luck won't solve.

Just think, all this debt, overhead,
and litigation from a little business
we started in my garage.

David, when are you going to accept the fact that daddy left this company to me? . . . and when you've typed the dictation, make a fresh pot of coffee.

I resigned over a policy conflict . . .
I wanted to stay but they wanted
me to leave.

Maybe we can charge for parking while they're at our gasoline pumps.

You may as well discontinue your
presentation . . . they've turned
down their hearing aids.

Chapter 3

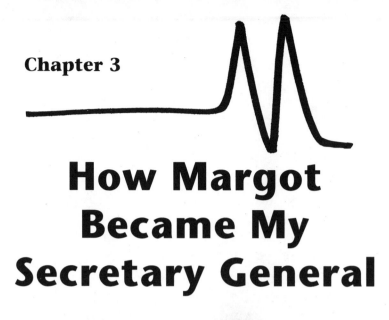

How Margot Became My Secretary General

Yes, I am a career girl
. . . you must be the career boys.

For years I referred to Margot as my secretary. That was the title she preferred. We had many discussions on the subject.

"Wouldn't you rather be my executive assistant, administrative assistant, or something fancier? 'Secretary' implies that you do secretary-like things, such as type, file, buy carbon paper, and. . . ."

"Although I can type 100 words-per-minute, flawlessly, I do no typing. Madeline does that with the word processing system. I manage all your schedules, balance your personal books, arrange travel, remind you of all important dates, do some purchasing, keep your tax records, screen your calls beautifully, prepare all your meeting and board agendas, and generally make you look good. Very good. And no one buys carbon paper," she responded.

"I also lie for you occasionally and don't like that. You may also recall that I am a member of Phi Beta Kappa, have a masters degree in art history, and possess teaching credentials."

"Wow! How does Human Resources classify you?"

"I am identified as an 'executive assistant' with qualifications in foreign languages, accounting, and other things extending far beyond what I have just told you." And with a cute smile she added, "And if the whole system wasn't so screwed up, I would probably have your job and you would have mine . . . although I'm not certain you could handle mine . . . you might be homeless."

"Are you absolutely sure you don't want a better title? Wouldn't it impress your husband?" I persisted.

"Not at all. I honestly prefer 'secretary.' The title sounds great to me. It has historical significance. There are secretaries of state, treasury, defense, agriculture, commerce, etc. . . . and don't overlook the 'secretary general' of the United Nations. Now that I reflect on it, I think I might prefer to be identified as 'secretary general' . . . but I have to go now . . . I have serious work to do and so do you."

Margot was kidding about "secretary general," but when she arrived at her desk the following Monday, she found a nice box of steel-die engraved business cards identifying her as "secretary general."

The cards cost $85 and were worth it.

You're good at so few things, why
don't you resign and become a
consultant.

I got tired of waiting
and made my own.

Your experience with failure is helping us through a very difficult period.

If our new compact is so great,
how come you still tool around in a
company limousine?

Have you considered the possibility
that it's the management problem
more than the recession problem?

My new executive assistant is
brilliant, creative, and tireless . . .
I've got to get rid of her.

I simply want you to treat me as though you were running for Congress and I represented the entire women's vote.

If you have any more
humble opinions, please
keep them to yourself.

Mrs. Weber . . . do you by chance
recall what I had in mind when I
bought this company?

You've got an ulcer? I didn't realize
that underachievers got ulcers.

Chapter 4

Laughing About Lawyers

Things are so slow with our attorneys,
they have decided to sue us.

The best way to deal with lawyers is to avoid them. Whatever it costs to avoid them will be less than it costs not to.

A lot is written about lawyers, most of it not very laughable. Popularity polls, depending on the public mood that day, rank them somewhere near junk bond kings. Warren Burger's observation is still correct: "We are on our way to a society overrun by hordes of lawyers, hungry as locusts." Technical details have become more important than right or wrong.

There are many fine lawyers who practice at the highest levels and make heroic attempts to manage good government, run great institutions, and help negotiate world peace. They rarely get the good press they deserve.

Some others are not so fine and many tired jokes on lawyers and the legal profession abound. Most lawyers laugh good naturedly at lawyer jokes and often tell them.

My favorite is about the 53-year-old lawyer who was greeted by Saint Peter with enormous fanfare because St. Peter, having audited his time sheets, thought he was admitting the first 900-year-old attorney.

My most unfavorite day of the month is when I examine attorney bills to determine whether their inspirational calculations of billable time are acceptable. Once I felt that most attorneys had a burning desire to save the world. Now I recognize that their burning desire has more to do with staying rich.

Medals for lawyers? Many distinguished lawyers deserve medals and ribbons for professional gallantry in action. But most don't. And there is a select group that qualifies

Young hard-billing lawyer telling lawyer joke to clients.

annually for the "Creative Billing Citation" for special creativity in jacking up charges by innovative utilization of word processing and photocopy equipment.

Closely associated with lawyers in the public's eyes are those celebrity "look-like-lawyers" who combine the qualities of statesman, economist, guru, negotiator, and media figure. They are authorities on all subjects, including the law, but aren't lawyers. They, too, can be good for healthy laughter.

Dr. Henry (Heinz) Alfred Kissinger, for example. Central casting would have him as a Supreme Court Justice or very senior partner. I recall sitting next to Henry on the grass at an out-

door band concert several years ago and observing that his fingernails had a chewed-to-the-quick look. Yikes! I watched the news closely for several days, wondering if some secret international crisis had reduced him to stubby fingernails. I sleep better when the president, my doctor, my banker, and my attorney aren't chewing their fingernails.

The list of those who have laughed, criticized, and written about lawyers is long, impressive, and growing longer. It is interesting that the most outspoken criticism comes from those who understand humor, use humor, and laugh at themselves. (And, to be fair, this group includes some fine lawyers.) Will Rogers, G. B. Shaw, Groucho Marx, and William Shakespeare were among the most colorful who villified and laughed at lawyers. Lawyers have been worked over since they were first invented. "A countryman between lawyers is like a fish between two hungry cats," is what Ben Franklin had to say.

Is it possible that all this criticism, bashing, and derisive laughter is a unique form of recognition and distinction? Unfortunately, in our system, I can't get along without lawyers and I wish I knew more judges.

The top line is our law firm . . .
the bottom line is us.

SMART CHART by Stansbury

Golly, Dennis . . . I don't think I've seen you since our firm represented you at the bankruptcy hearings.

I'm sorry we didn't win for you, Roger . . . but our young attorneys did appreciate the opportunity to get their first courtroom experience.

It's a bill from your attorney for the
free advice at lunch.

True, the legal profession isn't everything, son . . . but it does bring recognition, power, conquests, clubs, fast cars. . . .

SMART CHART

by Stansbury

For me it's never been the money . . . just the wonderful legal challenges.

They rip us, Harry, but each day I
give thanks that we are genuinely
selfish and greedy lawyers.

**True, our legal expenses were high
. . . but we did win the lawsuit.**

Frankly, I've always felt that living
beyond our means demonstrates
faith in the law.

Our attorneys Broderick, Kent, Simpson, Brotherton, Fenwald, Carrington, MacBride, Klein, and Cribbins are suing us. We got their name wrong.

My attorney is leaving his brain to
medical science . . . they want time
to think it over.

Chapter 5

My Good Buddies at the IRS

The IRS has discovered that Jack Daniels
is not my dependent uncle.

Last spring in San Francisco, sitting on the edge of the dock at Red's Java House on the Embarcadero, I noticed that my palms were unusually hot and moist as I washed down my double-dog with an ice-cold cherry Coke. I had no other symptoms. Just nervous, hot hands. Returning to the office, I almost let myself get nailed by a Muni bus at Market and Montgomery and then tripped on the wheelchair ramp in front of San Francisco Federal at Post and Kearny.

WHILE YOU WERE OUT, THE IRS CALLED... THEY QUESTION YOUR LUNCHEON WINE SELECTIONS FOR 1988 AND 1990.

Alzheimer's? A nervous disorder? Not at all. Just early signals of tax time proximity. It happens every year. The IRS makes me nervous. In their big computer, I prefer to be stored as an almost anonymous good friend.

My income is generated from a variety

of unrelated sources, a phenomenon that puzzles some examiners. They aren't certain what I do until I go through a complete show-and-tell. No one at the IRS ever told me that I don't fit in a traditional category, but I believe that is the problem. That's the message I sense.

"What kind of car do you drive? How can you draw cartoons that make fun of business and be a businessman? You made contributions to something called 'Bear Backers' and other weird things. I find all this terribly confusing."

The examiner stares at me, steely-eyed. I stare back, placidly. But it always works out OK. I've never been fined and any extra money I've paid over the years has been nominal. And sometimes they have even paid me.

Moreover, I want to go on record that the IRS people have always treated me with courtesy and friendliness. But even with their good manners, free coffee, and the presence of my accountant, an audit is a nervous event preceded by several weeks of stressful anticipation.

I don't like audits and I don't know anyone who can't be traumatized or at least brought to attention by an IRS audit. The sales manager of a large Los Angeles printing firm once told me that his field salespeople never read or reacted to his monthly "inspirational" memorandums. "They don't even open the envelopes," he complained. I suggested he try different envelopes. "Print some with an IRS return address. They'll open those."

I was kidding but later he told me the envelope strategy worked. The salespeople all opened their envelopes but did not appreciate the instant stress joke. I doubt if he'll seek further advice.

Overall, the IRS strategy looks this way: from New Years Day until April 15, they frighten people with lots of publicity about prominent individuals being jailed for tax evasion. Leona Helmsley was a perfect example a few years ago. Don't you imagine her case whipped a few folks into prompt alignment? The rest of the year, I believe, is spent creating incomprehensible tax instructions.

For the individual income tax, my vote is for a modest, uniform, flat tax rate or some kind of value-added tax. A fixed percentage of personal income. No deductions. No tax for those legitimately at the poverty level.

I particularly enjoy drawing IRS cartoons and I fantasize that someday the IRS will buy a few Smart Charts to lighten up the heavy load of tax instructions.

And wouldn't it be great to file an income tax return that listed the Internal Revenue Service as a source of income.

The ideal solution would be for the
post office to run the IRS and the
IRS to run the post office.

**It's from the IRS . . . They say
they've got you in their hip pocket.**

SMART CHART
by Stansbury

My doctor has advised me
to cut down on taxes.

The IRS auditors would never have
suspected a thing if I hadn't
laughed so hard just as they were
going out the door.

**Does the IRS send
accidental sinners to jail?**

I wonder how the IRS will respond
to your plea of temporary insanity.

The good news is we paid no
Federal taxes . . . the bad news is
we forgot to file.

The IRS is after me. They
won't allow the depreciation
I've been taking on my brain.

The IRS returned the candied
fruit. If it's all the same to you,
they prefer Glenlivet.

The IRS says we've made it
to the playoffs in the
creative fiction division.

The IRS didn't let me write off
my brandy purchases as a
charitable contribution to the
Christian Brothers.

SMART CHART
by Stansbury

The IRS wants to know
what business expenses you
included under "frivolity."

**The IRS has found rats
in our tax shelters.**

We spoke out against large
federal deficits . . . then the IRS
spoke out against ours.

A hearty welcome to our firm,
Fuller. Human Resources reported
that your father is a senior
executive with the IRS.

Chapter 6

What's New in Humanoid* Resources?

* I use the term "humanoid" because so much that comes out of human resources looks more humanoid than human. When they cease to invent and encourage dumb language, we can switch back.

Motivation is a popular agenda item at every level of business. It may be most popular for the Human Resource people. CEOs work on it. Shop foremen work on it. Parents, coaches, teachers, and generals work on it. It's impossible to locate someone who is not trying to motivate someone else.

How can Human Resources motivate? What things can be done to incite action, cause ignition, and inspire energetic drive?

SOME DAYS IT'S HARD TO GET MOTIVATED

Food could be a massive motivator in a starvation environment. In this country there are special recognition dinners and the various gift food packages for holidays, but food itself is rarely used.

Money is a useful motivator and works well most of the time. It can be a salary, a bonus, or a commission payment, dangled as a carrot or held back. It can go into a retirement fund or be the incentive for early retirement. The only problem with money is that it is often in short supply.

What about sex? I doubt if sex is on any approved human resource list, at least in the United States. Can you visualize a sales executive explaining the sales-sex bonus to a husband or wife?

Recognition is a form of respect and I see no end to its possibilities as a Human Resource device. Titles can sometimes substitute for money. The advertising and banking professions observed early that passing out vice presidencies works. In academia it's vice chancellorships.

At one time a salesman was simply a peddler or hawker, but much later he became a sales representative, account manager, account executive, assistant vice president, and a bunch of other things. Most garbage men are now waste disposal engineers.

Employee of the week, month, or year are recognitions which involve a plaque, and of course there are the various retirement awards conceived to inspire those who are left behind.

Respect may be the best motivator. Consciously or not, it is probably the most cherished. Respect from one's family, peers, team members, employers, and competitors conveys a wonderful emotion. How do you get

respect? How do you give it? The proper answers might call for a long philosophical discussion. But in the short form it simply means the Golden Rule. Treat your fellow humans exactly as you prefer to be treated. Human Resource experts need to work on this. People are not commodities and those who use terms like "downsize" should be banished.

The time has come for Human Resources to invent better schemes for recognizing fine performances by employees. Bonuses are fine and so are promotions. But the scientific, military, and athletic worlds are far ahead. The military has theater ribbons to reveal where a person has served. Shouldn't someone who has worked in Salinas, California get a Salinas ribbon? Imagine the thrill of meeting another Salinas veteran in Manhattan.

I know a distinguished chemist with 52 Honorary Doctorates and I know a halfback with more rings, trophies, medallions, and pins than he can count. A retired master sergeant has 37 ribbons and medals. But the vice president for sales at a big printing company has nothing more than his tarnished Rotary pin and a Silver Beaver Award from the Boy Scouts.

The military establishment seems to distribute a lot more medals and ribbons than it used to. Have you noticed on television, when a high-ranking officer is interviewed in uniform, the entire left side of his chest is usually blanketed with ribbons clear to the shoulder?

EARLY EGYPTIAN
MBA RECEIVES
HIS GOLDEN FLY

Medals and ribbons are wonderful devices for recognizing people and they don't cost much. In the days of Imperial China there were hat badges and peacock feather decorations. Egyptian pharaohs passed out golden flies.

In the business community, most executives settle for various pins, badges, and emblems . . . Rotary, athletic teams, flags, corporation logos, United Way, the Olympics, the Tournament of Roses, political candidates, and a wide variety of charities and other worthwhile causes.

Consider a special Human Resources medal for an heroic act of anti-nepotism for the young man who gets in there and forces out his grandfather, two uncles, and daddy, men who always insisted on running the corporation "their way." And there could be Survivor

Lapel Ornaments for those who withstood takeover assaults with a smile and Victory Medals for those who won playing the merger game.

Wouldn't it be a splendid idea to give business people the opportunity to receive medals and ribbons for exceptional acts of business heroism and courage. Awards for participation in high-risk financial ventures. Awards for those wonderful people who un-jam the copy machine. How about the Purple Pancreas Award for sales executives who are thrown out of customer's offices? And shouldn't there be a medal for those who simply stick around for years in dull, meaningless jobs?

HAROLD... THIS IS FOR YOUR 42 YEARS IN A DULL AND MEANINGLESS JOB.

There might also be the Team Player or Going Along ribbons for those dependable members of the board who can always be counted on to vote *your way* . . . those great pals who come forth with fast supporting motions. And don't overlook those who help nail things down with a fast second. There might even be an annual award for frequency of "quality motions."

Quiet acts of courage go on in business every day. Loyal yes-men and yes-women labor faithfully to reinforce our egos by dependably saying "Yes" with enthusiasm when we are in grave need of a yes. Isn't it time to recognize those unsung and frequently ridiculed heroes and heroines? Let's not call them brown nosers any longer.

Matching miniature medals for spouses would be popular and fabric ribbon sets for Velcro application to golf shirts, swimming trunks, or pajamas would set a trend.

Fortune 500 CEO, preparing to tee-off at the Cypress Point club, explains his decoration to attentive senior yes-men.

The possibilities seem infinite.

To conclude a recent retirement dinner, executive secretaries recommended these awards:

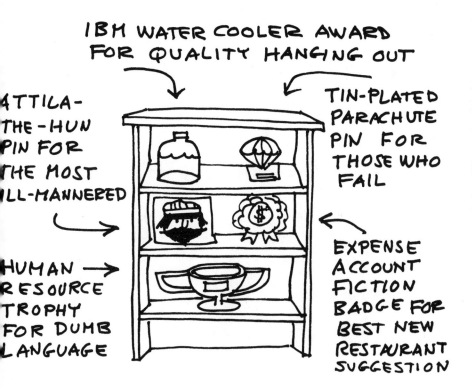

IBM WATER COOLER AWARD FOR QUALITY HANGING OUT

ATTILA-THE-HUN PIN FOR THE MOST ILL-MANNERED

TIN-PLATED PARACHUTE PIN FOR THOSE WHO FAIL

HUMAN RESOURCE TROPHY FOR DUMB LANGUAGE

EXPENSE ACCOUNT FICTION BADGE FOR BEST NEW RESTAURANT SUGGESTION

Humanoid Resources has barely scratched the surface of motivational opportunity.

You're being transferred to the
micro division, Mortensen . . .
you'll have a smaller desk, smaller
chair, smaller coffee cup.

Congratulations, Jay . . . it takes
some trainees five years to work up
from wimp to yes-man.

SMART CHART
by Stansbury

Congratulations, Dibble. Very few
of our new MBAs test as high on
materialism as you do.

In making your corporate career plans, Ferguson, we suggest you aspire to low middle-management.

SMART CHART
by Stansbury

Basically they liked your
resume and will keep you in mind
if they need a hall monitor.

Congratulations Dunbar. Human
Resources tells me you have developed
some genuine stress symptoms.

The tests reveal a modest IQ, no
aptitude for business, and great
skill as a liar . . . we suggest you
run for Congress.

No, Green, you're not
an insider . . . but you are a highly
regarded outsider.

The tests are conclusive
. . . you are entirely justified in
your feelings of inferiority.

I can't decide which is worse . . .
staying here and hating it, or going on
my own and risking starvation.

Perhaps we could discuss my raise
again at a later date, sir?

We can't afford a gold watch,
Dailey, but we are retiring your
coffee cup.

You are correct, Penrose . . .
last week when we announced the
merger, no personnel changes were
anticipated. This week they are.

Everyone likes you,
Butler . . . all that's stopping you
is bad luck and lack of ability.

Chapter 7

Born to Sell

Most people who become big shots in sales
and marketing were born with the sales gene.

Men and women who have had phenomenal sales and marketing success began their careers in sales and stayed there because it was instinctive. They had training along the way but it was the gut-feel instinct that made them succeed.

Half jokingly I told biophysics professor Cornelius Tobias that males born with sales gene locus 1565 on the Y chromosome would probably have successful sales careers. He laughed and said that my concept could be correct but he wasn't sure of the number. Then he added that females would have the same gene on the X chromosome.

CONGRATULATIONS ... YOUR BABY DAUGHTER HAS GENE LOCUS 1565 ON THE X CHROMOSOME. SHE WAS BORN TO SELL!

The subjects of "sales sense" and "sense of humor" are never comfortably explained unless the explainer and the explainee already possess them.

Sales instincts show up early in the form of the first lemonade stand, selling tickets door-to-door, summer jobs, baby-sitting, and part-time jobs in high school and college.

Successful salespeople are fun at parties, give better parties, stay up later, and are tolerant of human frailty. Today they don't drink much and most used to smoke.

They were initiated into sales after scoring well on interviews and screening hurdles, a visit to the home office, introductions to the inside staff, and some product training. A few months later they were turned loose in a territory under the supervision of an assistant sales manager.

They knocked on thousands of doors of ice-cold prospects located in places which were identified in no geography book. They spent hours in bleak waiting rooms with

THEY KNOCKED ON THE DOOR OF ICE-COLD PROSPECTS

cheerless receptionists they hoped to charm, only to be rejected by a half-drunk purchasing agent who gave them five minutes before pointing to the door.

Selling is a complicated and frequently misunderstood human endeavor. Salespeople are often stereotyped as good story-tellers with finely developed senses of humor. This is an accurate description of many, but not a universal truth.

Having been involved in sales and marketing activities most of my life, I have a tendency to say heroic things about salespeople as well as make fun of their antics. Good salespeople need steady reenforcement because of the emotional beatings they take from sustained exposure to customers. They may be paid well, but one never develops enough scar tissue to protect against fierce rejection. It goes with the job. An aggressive sales demeanor is often a thin veneer of protection.

My first boss was a macho-tough pussycat who talked tough, sold well, and wore expensive clothes. He was a salesman, not a sales manager, and from him I eventually learned names like Bally, Rolex, Laphroaig, Borsalino, and also how to tip. I'm not certain beginning salespeople get lectures like the one I got from Barney. When he called me in I expected a sophisticated discussion.

"You will never wear a sportscoat or go without a hat in San Francisco again! We'll go at noon for the hat. Ankle socks are out! Neither I nor anyone else is interested in seeing your shin bones when you cross your legs! You will manage to complete 15 sales calls, face-to-face, every damn day, and you will write your sales reports at night. Never use my secretary for anything. (I discovered

Barney—my first sales manager

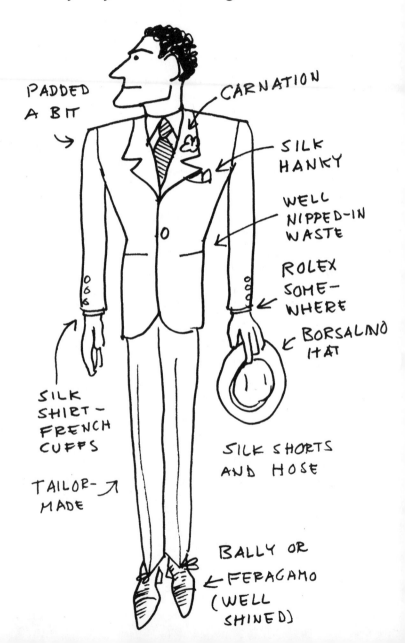

PADDED A BIT

CARNATION

SILK HANKY

WELL NIPPED-IN WASTE

ROLEX SOME-WHERE

BORSALINO HAT

SILK SHIRT — FRENCH CUFFS

TAILOR-MADE

SILK SHORTS AND HOSE

BALLY OR FERAGAMO (WELL SHINED)

later he was trying to have an affair with her.) Your monthly expense allowance is $50 and that's to entertain customers and get them slightly drunk. Learn to play golf, get on the golf committee at the San Francisco Advertising Club and if you have any problems, speak to me, not my secretary or corporate headquarters."

Crudely as it began, I learned a great deal about human equations from Barney. He was not who he seemed. He was worse. But for no reason I understand, I came to like him.

At a recent dinner for some blazing sales successes, I asked them to name one thing,

THE BLAZING SALES SUCCESSES GAVE ME THEIR CANDID ANSWERS.

big or little, that helped them succeed. I collected 39 responses. These six were my favorites:

1. Give goofy presents

now and then. To help a friend quit smoking I gave him $50 worth of bubble gum. He never quit talking about it. I have a client who loves Snickers. To her, $25 worth of Snickers means far more than a $25 bottle of wine.

2. Write notes

. . . especially thank you notes. I carry small, white postal size cards with colorful stamps . . . I try to select stamps that are on good topics. I write a one or two line note after *every* call. I address them in advance and scribble my notes while waiting for the elevator and I

mail instantly. I write
to suppliers who visit
me as well as customers and my own staff.

3. Start the day early.

Really early. Two or three hours early. I simply arise at the same time as the paper boy.
Those early hours are super-productive and it
all adds up to two extra days of production
each week. It screws up breakfast with the
family but I'm home by 6 p.m. (when I'm in
town). Having a paper route as a youngster is
a good way to get into the habit.

4. Entertain customers at breakfast . . .

group breakfast meetings instead of lunch or
dinner. Great breakfasts at nice places are not
expensive and avoid the cocktail issue. Sometimes I bring a celebrity in politics, sports,
media, a minister, rabbi, or priest. I often pass
out samples of our products and arrange for
others to do the same thing. I'm famous for
my breakfasts. I sell running shoes.

5. Remain humble forever.

Thank those who criticize you constructively, even though they handle it poorly. Don't ever terminate or transfer someone if their offensive criticism is accurate. Nerds who do this are valuable but it's a good idea to keep them away from customers or important members of your team who might be disrupted. It is difficult to find quality critics who are not offensive. It is important to recognize their value and capitalize on it . . . even though your instinct is to terminate them.

NOBODY LIKES CRITICISM...CONSTRUCTIVE OR ANY OTHER KIND. LISTEN ANYWAY.

6. Bring home presents

to your spouse, even if you've been gone only two days. See's candy at the airport on the way home works well. Bring the out-of-town

BRING HOME A
PRESENT

paper . . . at least the Sports section if your kids are athletically inclined.

Good salespeople often are loners, highly organized, and slightly introverted. They work long hours and don't always reveal much. The image of a gregarious, back-slapping, story-telling extrovert is rarely accurate. The day of the drummer was long ago.

My favorite salespeople have a sense of humor, laugh at themselves, work with great focused energy, and have plenty of laughter left over to share with others.

$

You're a real scumbag,
Bradshaw . . . I love that quality
in a sales trainee.

SMART CHART
by Stansbury

Stanford Business School is
building a case study around my
entertainment receipts.

Did their purchasing agent mention anything besides your hair and bad breath?

SMART CHART
by Stansbury

Ace Clifford wants a bigger
office . . . something more
suitable for chip shots.

**Try to think of it as a minor change
in your corporate title . . .
from Vice President Sales to
Former Vice President Sales.**

Does your wife still believe I'm a purchasing agent from Omaha?

You've got it backwards, Henderson . . .
successful executives talk golf at the
office and business on the golf course.

Golly, Suzanne . . . I never dreamed
that one day I'd be an item on *your*
expense account.

We realize that you've broken every
sales record three years in a row,
Albert . . . but just for the heck of it, let
me tell you a little bit about our
corporate dress code.

Your sales performance is
fine . . . but you have an identity
problem . . . I'm your father and I can't
remember your name.

SMART CHART
by Stansbury

He's not much of a salesman but he's our number one marathon runner.

Your Stanford MBA and Yale
Doctorate are great, Randy . . . but
you've still got to sell your monthly
quota of kitty litter.

Our sales Vice President likes us to
remember he's descended from an
Irish king.

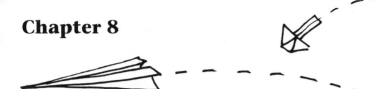

Chapter 8

How Chief Financial Officers Relieve Executive Boredom

How do they relax?
Perhaps the same way you do.

Several years ago, late on a cold autumn day following a long meeting of financial officers, a group gathered in my room at the Sherry Netherland in Manhattan. They had shared a long day and now cared only to relax and sip some of my single-malt scotch.

A young CFO perked up and said, "Let's have a paper airplane contest. We can compete for distance and time aloft. We're high enough, it's stopped sleeting, and these windows open wide."

It was obvious we were being sucked into competition with an expert.

The window was wide open now and everyone was on their knees manufacturing airplanes. The young CFO was folding the front page of the *Wall Street Journal* into what he identified as the Financial Officer Gull Wing.

In a few minutes, the fine financial minds of ten young men and women had created the first fleet of competitive entries in The Sherry Netherland International Paper Airplane Trophy Race.

The event was exciting and reminded me of similar competitions in our advertising and sales team meetings years earlier. These people weren't counting beans or pushing pencils... they were acting like sales executives. Even those that didn't know Knockando Scotch were sipping mine rapidly.

In your mail room or executive suite there are skilled men and women who can fabricate these:

EXECUTIVE SECRETARIAL DART

CHIEF FINANCIAL OFFICER GULL WING

BOARDROOM BOMBER
(FOLDED FROM LARGE KRAFT ENVELOPE FROM ACCOUNTING REPORT)

FAX FIGHTER
(OLD-FASHIONED PLAYGROUND "LOOPER")

SPORTS SECTION FLOATER
(LARGE GLIDER, SLOW FLYING, IDEAL FOR STADIUM ENTERTAINMENT)

We considered a race but finally agreed only to compete for time aloft and distance. The winner would get a free dinner. The CFO's Gull Wing shot toward Central Park, but a stray gust caught it and it crashed upside down with its wings pathetically bent, soaking wet, on the hotel canopy below.

I landed one helicopter well into Central Park and the other on the steps of the Plaza Hotel. My choppers were made from the high-quality, high-rag-content hotel stationery. One stayed up 37 seconds and I won both events.

My wife Audrey got after me for littering, but I explained that I was distributing corporate good humor because of the cartoons I had drawn on the wings.

Jim Davy, my former business partner, and I used to meet regularly at our San Francisco office, years earlier, for similar events. On Friday afternoons in our Sutter Street offices, we dropped paper helicopters in clusters. His were yellow and mine were white. We released our squadrons at the same time and the first chopper to reach Market Street won. The loser bought a round at the Pied Piper in the Palace Hotel.

This is how they are made:

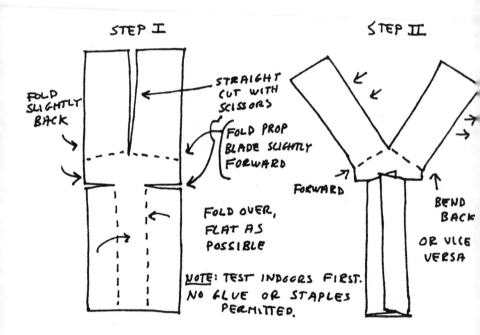

STEP I

FOLD SLIGHTLY BACK

STRAIGHT CUT WITH SCISSORS

FOLD PROP BLADE SLIGHTLY FORWARD

FOLD OVER, FLAT AS POSSIBLE

NOTE: TEST INDOORS FIRST. NO GLUE OR STAPLES PERMITTED.

STEP II

FORWARD

BEND BACK

OR VICE VERSA

This is the basic Stansbury helicopter. The size indicated works well. Quality hotel stationery is perfect. Nice weight. Dropped from a high building, the little choppers really spin, and when a warm, rising current or updraft comes along, they climb and can travel miles, often out of sight. I like to believe they eventually land in the ocean and dissolve.

Archimedes, roughly in 215 B.C., in Sicily, discovered the principle of floating in air. Ballooning came 2000 years later. The modern male business executive "plays" with flying throughout life, is fascinated by it, and sometimes relies on the corporate jet as a supremacy symbol. His sustained interest in flight from youth through old age has been documented for centuries.

The aeronautical virus remains with most business executives and today there are among us those who still enjoy a paper airplane toss,

especially from a high building. But it is difficult, today, to find windows in executive suites and boardrooms that open. That fact coupled with more rigidly enforced littering laws diminishes opportunities for this kind of recreation.

Paper airplanes remain popular but there are many ways for chief financial officers to relieve boredom. My research suggests that what they do is not unique . . . that what they do is shared by employees at all levels. CFOs have a much greater capacity for boredom because they are so immersed in long meetings and lots of important numbers. They resort to the same antics as the marketing people, but less frequently. Their jobs demand that they pay attention.

CFOs toss or flip wadded paper balls no differently than the sales vice president.

THREE POINTS!

Because steel-spring clamps are used to hold thick reports together, good rubber bands are vanishing. The rubber band was the best all-around propulsion medium in existence . . . you could propel the rubber band itself, or use it for the high-speed propulsion of small paper wads or dangerous, pain-inflicting paper-clip missiles.

One of my directors recently constructed an interesting big clamp sculpture which eventually became unsprung and sent clamps flying in all directions.

During the past few months I've kept notes and drawn sketches of chief financial officers in their efforts to relieve boredom, especially in boardrooms. CFOs are called on for long reports and extensive listening.

Generally speaking, their techniques don't vary much from other executives, but they conceal it better.

Paper airplanes

Not common. Late in day, usually. A group activity. Don't do it alone.

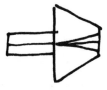

Upside-down reading practice

Easy to do without detection. The *Wall Street Journal* can be read in pieces if properly obscured by financial reports and other props.

Paper-clip jumper

Compress arm A behind arm B. Tricky. Tension holds for a minute and then arms spring apart and clip leaps three feet in air.

This is my favorite and a guaranteed disrupter. Use it when the speaker is hopeless and has gone on much too long. Requires some practice to perfect. Paper clips are extremely popular for small-wire sculpture, the common chain necklace, and as an ineffective device for nail cleaning.

Swapping Doodles

This is an old faithful and must be done discreetly with a pal who enjoys it as much as you do. It has the potential for severe board disruption.

Other boredom-relief activities

- Pretending to take serious notes while working on a more interesting project
- Tearing a piece of paper into the smallest possible pieces
- Trying to fold a piece of paper in half as many times as possible (the maximum number is seven no matter how large the sheet you start with)
- Bending a beverage bottle cap into a weird shape
- Practicing multiplication tables up to 15
- Playing calculator number games
- Private doodling
- Making spit balls (old fashioned but it still goes on)

CHIEF FINAN-
CIAL OFFICER
SUBCONSCIOUSLY
MAKING SPITBALL
FROM COVER PAGE OF MARKETING VICE-
PRESIDENT'S STRATEGIC PLAN. THIS
ACTUALLY HAPPENED.

Boredom relief is not limited to chief financial executives. It takes place at every business level, is rarely discussed, and will never be an agenda item.

But it is an honest activity, a healthy release, and part of a good-natured system for getting at the truth.

There's no dissension in the accounting department . . . we all signed the petition to have you fired.

The real question facing us is
whether to declare bankruptcy . . .
or embezzle the remaining assets.

At midyear we introduced the new accounting system . . . in reality we're still insolvent.

We have entered a period of great economic stability . . . We aren't losing money, we aren't making money.

Our Chief Financial Officer has a great track record . . . they know him at Santa Anita, Belmont, Hollywood Park. . . .

We may have a bank problem . . . their
last calendar was for only six months.

Do either of you recall where we
hid our hidden assets?

Stupid Stanley absconded with all the liabilities.

Aside from the accounting irregularities, misleading statements, and inventory manipulation, did the auditors have anything else to say?

The only thing we know for sure is
that our controller withdrew
60 grand the day of the race.

Occasional dipping into petty cash is not a fringe benefit.

Our strategy was to
hit bottom and bounce.

SMART CHART
by Stansbury

Every time we manage to
balance one thing, we
unbalance something else.

Last year, we emphasized
borrowing. This year, we will
emphasize borrowing some more.

I didn't realize what serious
shape the government was in until
my income tax refund bounced.

We figured that after the merger
combined earnings would go up.

First the good news . . . . we're
going to be on the covers of
Fortune, Forbes, Business Week
and page one of the *Wall Street
Journal.*

Maybe God didn't intend that all MBAs become CEOs overnight.

Chapter 9

The Last Laugh

We began to laugh at ourselves
and tell it like it really is.

Letting straight talk and laughter be distributed from the boardroom throughout the organization produces a leavening comfort when things are going wrong . . . or right.

Healthy laughter contains enormous integrity, courage, and fearlessness that enables us to go ahead at full throttle.

Good humor and truth go hand-in-hand with power, leadership, and authority, for all these qualities are symptoms of a strength of character and fitness of purpose that make business so much fun.

A sense of humor may not yet be a prerequisite for top executive positions, but it should be.

The Author

 standing joke among those who know Herb Stansbury well is that no one can figure out what he really does for a living. What is Herb's main thing? College roommate Don Mitchell says, "We don't know exactly what Herb does, but he seems to do it very well."

Herb Stansbury is difficult to tag with a single label, although an astrologist who sat next to him on United, flying east, told Herb he was a classic Scorpio without knowing his birthday is November 12.

The media has called him many things—"Undisputed King of Corporate Humor," "Fortune 500 Speaker," "Marketing Magician," and "Bohemian." But there is more.

Herb is chairman of San Francisco Federal Savings, a $3.5 billion savings and loan (a successful one), chairman of one other corporation, and director of two others. He is asked to consult and speak frequently.

For 15 years he produced Smart Chart, a widely syndicated business cartoon distributed by the *Los Angeles Times*. He doodles constantly, and it is impossible to estimate the number of friends and strangers who have salvaged the random cartoon art he drew on menus, napkins, envelopes, and boardroom scraps.

He began cartooning seriously in 1946 when he won a contest to become cartoon editor of the University of California's *Daily Californian*. His panel was called "Bearing Down." Today, nearly a half century later, Herb still keeps close ties to the University of California bears.

He is an enthusiast for worthwhile causes, and they are numerous. The University of California at Berkeley is probably highest on his list—The Department of Intercollegiate Athletics (Bear Backer fundraising), Lawrence Berkeley Laboratory (The Libra cancer research project), Lawrence Hall of Science (Dinosaurs) and Bancroft Library (Mark Twain).

Nobel Laureate Glenn Seaborg points out that Herb was very interested in science until he was severely challenged by advanced mathematics. "Actually, it wasn't that advanced," Herb laughs. "I hated calculus and my Russian professor couldn't speak understandable English. But I'm great at arithmetic."

Besides the Berkeley bears, Herb's other worthwhile causes include counseling young people beginning their careers, helping older people find employment, and encouraging people of all ages who need encouragement. He also paints occasionally and collects British and American cartoon and illustration art. For the California Academy of Sciences, he created a family of comic dinosaurs.

Although Herb was once an editor, publisher, and sales promotion executive with Miller Freeman, Inc., this is his first book. The manuscript was literally written and illustrated with an Expresso medium point (.5mm) pen. Herb owns a Macintosh and two ancient Underwoods but he prefers to hand-letter his text.

"Now you have your answer," Herb grins. "I write, draw, do business, try to raise money for worthwhile causes, pretend to be a scientist, paint, help people when I can, and talk. That's about it."

Herb is relaxed, good natured, viscerally motivated, and lives cheerfully with his wife, Audrey, in upscale Piedmont, California. Audrey is an active community leader and their two married daughters, Kimberly Blue and Lindsey Meyersieck, follow successful business careers in San Francisco.

In describing Herb, scientist William R. Hewlett may have portrayed him most accurately with his reflective insight:

"Anyone who knows Herb Stansbury knows what to expect. He has a delightful way of making you look at yourself as you appear to others. The art of humor is a friendly gig— just a nudge and never a push. In these skills, Herb excels."